WHERE DO WE
GO FROM HERE?

WHERE DO WE GO FROM HERE?

Hope and direction in our present crisis

Erwin W. Lutzer

MOODY PUBLISHERS
CHICAGO

© 2013 by
Erwin W. Lutzer

All Scripture quotations are taken from the *Holy Bible, New International Version*®, NIV®. Copyright ©1973, 1978, 1984, 2011 by Biblica, Inc.™ Used by permission of Zondervan. All rights reserved worldwide. www.zondervan.com

Interior design: Ragont Design
Cover design: Kathryn Duckett
Cover image: George Peters / 2008 iStock

ISBN: 978-0-8024-1013-9

We hope you enjoy this book from Moody Publishers. Our goal is to provide high-quality, thought-provoking books and products that connect truth to your real needs and challenges. For more information on other books and products written and produced from a biblical perspective, go to www.moodypublishers.com or write to:

Moody Publishers
820 N. LaSalle Boulevard
Chicago, IL 60610

1 3 5 7 9 10 8 6 4 2

Printed in the United States of America

It's gone.

Some of you will remember when the Christian philosopher Francis Schaeffer told us back in the 1970s that someday we would wake up and find out that the America we once knew was gone. *That day is here.*

We have crossed an invisible line, and there are no signs that we are capable of turning back. Like a boat caught in the mighty torrent of the Niagara River, we are being swept along with powerful cultural currents that just might put us over the brink. Seemingly irrevocable trends put in motion forty years ago continue to gather greater momentum and speed. Our Judeo-Christian heritage that gave us the freedoms we have enjoyed is for the most part gone, and in its place is an intolerant form of humanism that can boast of one victory after another. The "cultural war" we used to speak about appears to be over, and we have lost.

Daily, perhaps hourly, we are losing the war for America's heart and mind. We must understand the direction and speed of this cultural river that has spilled over and engulfed our land. We must also ask: what should we be doing at this critical hour?

This booklet is above all a message of hope, a message intended *to help us refocus our priorities in a day of great opportunity*. Rather than lick our wounds, withdraw from the public debate, and stand aside as we bemoan the fate of this great nation, we must regroup, get our bearings, and remember why we are here and what we are called to do. Never before in American history has it been more important for the church to be all that it can be in a society that is increasingly hostile to Christian values.

My prayer is that after you have finished reading these pages, you will be encouraged, hopeful, and excited to be alive at this moment of history. We as a church must embrace our present challenges with the sure knowledge that we are here by divine appointment. We have come to a crisis for which we must be prepared. We have work to do.

Before I seek to give both hope and direction to the church at this time of uncertainty, we need to survey the extent of the moral and spiritual devastation we see around us. Let's look at where we *are* before we outline what we should *do*.

There are at least five seemingly irreversible

trends in our society that we as a church must be prepared to address. I have no doubt that God is taking us where we have never been before, but He is not taking us where His grace cannot keep us.

Here I simply list these trends with a brief explanation.

FIVE TROUBLING TRENDS

Economic Decline

Even as I write these words, our ticking national debt clock tells us that we are increasing our debt by 3 billion dollars a day. We hear repeatedly that the 16 trillion dollars we owe nationally is "unsustainable"; that is to say, we cannot continue along this path of spending without drastic and long-term consequences. Our politicians have not yet learned that *we cannot borrow our way into prosperity and survive.*

Although there are many differences between America and post–World War I Germany, history has some economic lessons to teach us. Remember that after World War I, Germany was saddled with huge debts the nation chose to pay through the printing of money, and more money. Not everyone was hurt as a result of this strategy; businesses with huge debts paid them off with essentially worthless pieces of paper. The result, of course, was rapid inflation until the mark became worthless, and many people's savings were wiped out. The resulting economic collapse paved the way for a strong leader who promised to end the madness, and thus Hitler rose to power.

As of this moment I cannot predict what the long-term consequences of our spending binge will be, but most economists not only predict inflation (which is already happening) but possibly a severe recession, just as we witness one country after another in Europe struggling with high unemployment, wary investors, and the need for multibillion dollar bailouts. Yet because cutbacks are unpopular, Washington turns a deaf ear to the lessons of history.

Alexander Fraser Tyler, an eighteenth-century Scottish lawyer who was skeptical of democracy, ominously predicted:

> A democracy cannot exist as a permanent form of government. It can only exist until the voters discover that they can vote themselves largesse from the public treasury. From that moment on, the majority will always vote for candidates promising the most benefits from the public treasury with the result that

democracy always collapses over bad fiscal policy, always followed by a dictatorship.

We can be glad when the government helps the truly needy. But when elections are won or lost depending on which candidate promises the greatest "largesse," then we know that democracy is failing us. And when politicians are willing to keep increasing our national debt for immediate gain without regard for long-term consequences, then we know that we have lost our way.

Of course, it is not simply our national debt that should be of concern to us. Those of us who live in the state of Illinois are probably aware that the per-person debt in our state is among the highest in the nation. To be precise, our state is in debt to the tune of $21,000 for every person in Illinois! With the state treasury bankrupt, payments are either late or not paid at all.[1] A day of reckoning is coming.

My concern about the nation's economy is not just the effect a serious recession (or collapse) would have within our borders. Just think of America's global economic impact; then think of all the missionary organizations and agencies funded by American Christians. These sources of income, so desperately needed for the cause of the Gospel overseas, would dry up, and many Gospel-centered ministries would suffer around the world.

In anticipation of coming financial upheaval, we as a church should be grappling with relevant questions and design strategies that will help us care for those who are in need. The early church faced an economic crisis and helped its most under-resourced members. Our pride in our individualism must give way to a spirit of generosity, sharing, and sacrifice. We may have to learn such lessons the hard way.

Moral Decline

President Obama would not have pledged his support for same-sex marriage if he did not believe that in recent years there has been a massive public shift in cultural mores. Again, I refer to Francis Schaeffer, who warned us that what is unthinkable in one generation can become thinkable in another. What this moral shift toward the acceptance of same-sex marriage means for our children and succeeding generations is frightening.

The media has played an important role in making the unthinkable, thinkable. Pro-homosexual lobbies have exerted pressure and control to make sure that homosexuality is consistently portrayed in a favorable light, disregarding all its negative practices and consequences. In effect, the homosexual lobby has veto power over anything that is portrayed or said in the media about the gay lifestyle. The strategy of the radical homosexual movement is simple: *preach tolerance but practice intolerance at every opportunity*.

Meanwhile, schoolchildren are being indoctrinated in the acceptance of the normalcy of homosexuality. Faith-based adoption agencies have already had to close because they were being forced to adopt children to same-sex couples, in violation of their religious convictions. If a bill such as ENDA (Employment Non-Discrimination Act) were to become law, not even Christian organizations could discriminate in their hiring practices.

That said, it is important for us to realize that there are many within our churches who struggle with same-sex attraction, and we gladly welcome them into our churches. We as a church are called to live with the tension of both accepting the scriptural understanding of homosexuality and also dealing redemptively with all who struggle with any form of sexual immorality, whether fornication, adultery, or pornography and the like.

Those who come with a spirit of repentance, seeking forgiveness, healing, and help, should know that they are welcome among us.

The list of sins both outside the church and inside the church is growing. To drugs, alcohol, and sex, we can now add more recent addictions such as video games, the Internet, and social media. As Neil Postman warned nearly three decades ago, we are "amusing ourselves to death."

It is estimated that 60 percent of all pornography falls into the hands of children. Considering that this is a multibillion dollar industry, there is simply no way to estimate the damaging effects this flood of impurity continues to have as it spills into our culture.

We must ask: how do we as a church balance our condemnation of sin with a redemptive attitude that humbly acknowledges that the sins of the nation have become our sins? And, how can we best oppose those who would want to indoctrinate our children in various forms of immorality—and yet at the same time be known for our love and care for people who need to know the forgiveness of Christ?

As we sink into a moral morass, our role is difficult, but not impossible. Just ask the Christians in ancient Corinth who at times succeeded in their struggles against the sins of their culture but also at times failed. Their battle is our battle, and we had better not pretend our church is exempt from these sins. Christians are not always winners but they are always fighters, battling against sin. We can be encouraged to know that the church has been down this road before.

Educational Breakdown

Speaking of moral decline, our public schools have, for the most part, become government schools; often they are places of indoctrination for the nation's degrading values: homosexuality, premarital sex, and atheistic evolution. Sex classes are held that break down the natural resistance that young people have to sexual intimacy by teaching them how to have sex without having a baby or feeling guilty.

Recently, a volunteer here at Moody Church told us that in her daughter's school students were asked to choose sides in a classroom. On one side were the students who claimed to be gay and those who supported their lifestyle. On the other side were the bullies. Now, her daughter was forced to decide: should she join the bullies or should she walk over and endorse the gay lifestyle? Stories of how our children are being forced to affirm the homosexual lifestyle can be found in virtually any public school. And sadly, parents are often told that they have no input or control over the content of the curriculum.

Enough has been written elsewhere about the crisis in America's schools for parents to be educated about the cultural and moral philosophies intended to shape the thinking of our youth.[2] What the church must be doing is to be both empowering and instructing parents how to protect their children from the kind of indoctrination that is purposefully imposed on so many of our nation's children.

Prejudicial Legal Rulings

Ever since the Supreme Court, without constitutional authority, legalized abortion for any reason or no reason, judicial rulings have frequently become more arbitrary and prejudicial, often violating respect for religious freedom. Today, the First Amendment is turned on its head and the establishment clause is interpreted to mean that every expression of Christianity in the so-called public square violates the constitution. Organizations such as the ACLU have done all within their power to intimidate believers, forcing them to privatize their faith.

Elane Photography, a photography studio in New Mexico, was fined $7,000 for refusing, on religious grounds, to photograph a commitment ceremony for a same-sex couple. In 2008 the New Mexico Court of Appeals upheld the ruling of the New Mexico Human Rights Commission that the studio had violated the state's non-discrimination law.[3] In numerous cases, when homosexual rights and religious rights conflict, homosexual rights win.

This attitude of marginalizing those who hold to traditional values spills over into the public sphere. Who would have dreamed that the mayor of Chicago would declare that he would prohibit a business whose founders support traditional marriage from being able to set up a franchise in the city?[4] In October 2012, Angela McCaskill was suspended as an administrator from Gallaudet University for signing a petition to put Maryland's same-sex marriage legislation on the November ballot. In other words, even such an innocuous act, interpreted as questioning the right of same-sex couples to marry, is enough to cause suspension. Incredibly, the university justified its decision because of its view of *tolerance*![5]

As a church we must not be intimidated by the threats and actions of those who would want us to keep our faith to ourselves. When believers in the book of Acts were told that they should not preach in the name of Jesus, they continued to proclaim His Name even though it meant prison. Our challenges are not new; new to us yes, but not new to our brothers and sisters throughout the ages.

The Privileged Position of Islam

While biblical Christianity is in decline and often vilified, Islam will continue to enjoy a privileged position in politics and among a good percentage of the masses. For years the OIC (the Organisation of Islamic Cooperation) has tried to get the United Nations to approve an amendment regarding "defamation of religion." If this universal blasphemy law were approved, it would mean that all criticism of Islam would be criminalized. Fueled by incidents such as a Qur'an burning and a video that evidently ridiculed Muhammad, Muslims are demanding that nothing should ever be said or done that would be offensive to Islam.

Americans make a mistake when they judge Islam by its more tolerant American version. If we want to see what Islam is like as a religion, we must judge it by countries where it is in control: Saudi Arabia and Iran to name two. The laws of Saudi Arabia, for example, explicitly stipulate that converts from Islam to Christianity are to be executed. Also, in Islamic countries Christians are often put to death for "dishonoring Islam" not because they have spoken against it but simply because they believe in the Trinity, and this in itself is an insult to Islam.

Europe, which has a greater Muslim population than the United States, has, for the most part, forfeited any right to criticize Islam. Choosing to self-censor, politicians speak only favorably of Islam; to do otherwise would mean that they would be demonized by the media and the "politically correct" population as a whole. Meanwhile in Europe and now increasingly in the United States, crosses are being removed from hospitals and churches so as not to offend Muslims. And more serious concessions are being made in educational textbooks, the media, and in finance. Since the Quran teaches that Islam must establish itself as a superior religion, the concessions we make are but the first steps in a larger agenda. All of this poses a great challenge to the church in the coming years.[6]

However, as Christians we must never, not for a moment, entertain hatred for Muslims; indeed, when we understand their record on women's rights, for example, and the fear of apostasy that exists in Muslim communities, we should have a burden for them to come to know the forgiveness and grace of Christ. Once again, we are called to be the church: witnessing, welcoming, discerning, and standing for the truth of the Gospel in every way. We must intentionally educate our congregations so that believers will be prepared to make difficult decisions as they are faithful to the Gospel, and yes, gladly suffer for the cause of Christ as the need arises.

THE SLAUGHTER OF THE INNOCENTS

Proof that we as a nation must return to God was vividly demonstrated in the horrific crime committed at the Sandy Hook Elementary School in Newtown, Connecticut. When we think of the carnage of these precious children and their teachers and administrators, there are no words to describe the horror. Together we weep as individuals and as a nation.

"Where was God?" many people are asking. An interesting question in light of the fact that we have excised Him from our classrooms, law, government, and science. Indeed, He is not welcome anywhere in the so-called public square. And now when we need Him—when we see the horror of unflinching evil—we now ask where He is.

God is shouting to all who are willing to listen. In every heart there is the good and the bad: we have the shooter, and, in stark contrast, the first-grade teacher who was willing to take a bullet to protect the children in her classroom. Soviet dissident and Christian writer Aleksandr Solzhenitsyn brilliantly summarized our condition: "The line separating good and evil passes not through states, nor between classes, nor between political parties, but right through every human heart." Yes, there is evil, not just in the worst of us, but also in the best of us. What happened in Newtown is a powerful reminder that human nature is flawed and capable of unlimited evil.

As our nation drifts away from God, prayer, and moral decency, more people will choose to settle their disputes with violence to get "justice." As I write, crime is out of control here in Chicago. Our politicians are scrambling in their search for answers, blaming the economy, drugs, and guns. But ultimately, we need look no further than the human heart to find an answer to the question, "Why?" Despite the social factors that may make crime more appealing, ultimately people commit crimes because they *want* to.

We desperately need God, not just to explain evil but to combat it.

The prophet declared, "I will cleanse you . . . I will give you a new heart and put a new spirit in you; I will remove from you your heart of stone and give you a heart of flesh. And I will put my Spirit in you and move you to follow my decrees and be careful to keep my laws" (Ezekiel 36:25–27).

Thankfully, God has done something about evil. He has provided a Savior who can "save us from our sins."

In that confidence . . . where do we go from here?

A HISTORICAL PERSPECTIVE

For 2,000 years the church has almost always existed under political regimes and cultures that were hostile to the Christian message. We immediately think of the persecutions that Christians endured throughout the Roman Empire during the early centuries. Believers were not tortured because they believed in Jesus; in Rome one was free to believe in whatever god he wished. What galled the Romans was that Christians believed that *Christ was the only true God*. And because Christians were not willing to confess "Caesar is Lord" they were seen as politically subversive. Though some compromised their convictions, most stood for their faith. Countless thousands were put to death because they believed that some things were more important than blending in with the controlling ideas of their generation.

Some Christians reasoned that it would be advantageous if they had political power. Then they could use the sword to impose Christian beliefs on society as a whole. After Constantine became emperor in AD 306, Christianity became the official religion of the Roman Empire. Church and state were united; in fact, by the eighth century the state was under the authority of the church. When the pope crowned Charlemagne in Saint Peter's Basilica on Christmas day, AD 800, the authority of the church was uncontested.

As the church grew in power its corruption increased. Its political, religious, and moral decay was so pervasive that many true believers tried to break away from the church's authority. For this they were persecuted—many were drowned or killed with the sword. The true church insisted that with the coming of Constantine nothing had changed. In the early centuries they were put to death by the Romans and now centuries later they were put to death by the officials of Christendom. Either way, *they were a minority who elicited hostility from the cultural, ecclesiastical, and political powers of their time.*

Why do we think it should be different for us? Must we think that the church can survive only in those countries that are tolerant of the Christian message? Even in our day, have we forgotten Russia, Romania, and China? The church survived in these countries without any political power at all. The consistent lesson of 2,000 years of church history is that *the church does not need freedom to be faithful.*

Read almost any of the epistles in the New Testament, and you will be reading a message to a church that was in the throes of some kind of persecution. Whether at Corinth, Philippi, Ephesus, or the scattered groups to whom 1 Peter was written—all of those believers were trying to be authentically Christian in a pagan culture. The author of the book of Hebrews chided his readers by comparing their suffering with that of Christ and the martyrs. He wrote, "In your struggle against sin, you have not yet resisted to the point of shedding your blood" (Hebrews 12:4). He reminded them that, though they thought times were tough, they had not yet paid the ultimate price for faithfulness.

God is humbling the American church. In the early eighties we looked to the Moral Majority to halt our moral and spiritual toboggan slide. We thought our hope lay in the Congress, in the courts, in the White House. Evangelicals, we were told, held the balance of power. We could elect anyone we wanted, lobby for any laws we thought were right, and use the ballot box to tell the country that "we aren't going to take it anymore."

Throughout the nineties and the first decade of the new century, the church has taken a more chastened approach, quite aware that politics cannot restore biblical values to a culture that had cut its teeth on relativism, sexual freedom, and ballooning government entitlement programs. And, given the trends in more recent years, I've spoken to some Christians who are ready to throw up their hands and abandon any political involvement altogether.

We must be careful to not let the pendulum swing from one extreme to the other. Most assuredly, politics cannot save us—and yet it would be shortsighted to give up the political fight. We must rather understand what politics can and cannot do. We must remember Wilberforce's long and eventually victorious political fight against slavery, and Martin Luther King Jr.'s long and arduous battle against racial injustice, which resulted in important civil rights laws. Politics has an important role to play, but, needless to say, it will always fall short of the transformation of the human heart that our nation so desperately needs.

We should be thankful that the church has been awakened to the need to be involved in politics. But we must not be deluded—politics cannot save us. Politics is based on numbers, and numbers are based on coalitions that quickly fall apart when other issues become important. As the late Chuck Colson used to tell us, if we live by the political sword, we must die by it.

Let us humbly admit that America's lost Christian heritage cannot be reclaimed through government. If there is any truly good news in America, it will not be announced in Washington but will be heard through the lips and lives of believers who share the good news of the Gospel wherever God has planted them.

Our task, quite simply, is to witness to the truth of the Gospel in a nation that is under judgment. Someday there may be a cataclysmic reckoning, but we are paying for our sins right now. When God told Israel that disobedience would have severe consequences, He ended by saying, "Your sons and your daughters will be given to another nation, and you will wear out your eyes watching for them day after day, powerless to lift a hand" (Deuteronomy 28:32). The severest judgment was the scattering of Israel's families.

Though in a different way, the same is happening in America today. One-half of all children born this year will live with only a single parent, and the statistics within the church are not much better. The emotional scars left on our children will be passed on to the next generation. Today sons are crying for their fathers; daughters are crying for their mothers. Wives are filled with rage and men with hatred. The full effects of our disobedience will spill into an ever-widening flood in generations to come.

Should we collapse in despair, wring our hands, and give up? Shall we retreat from the world of politics, art, journalism, and education? Shall we sell our assets and go into hiding, waiting for the end of the world? No, God has left us here to be change agents; He has work for us to do. This is a wonderful opportunity for the church to be the church. This is a time that calls for courage and commitment that is worthy of the God we serve.

We must cling to what is unmovable in an age when everything that has been nailed down is being torn up. We must be as faithful as those who have gone before us.

Where *do* we go from here?

FIVE UNSHAKABLE PILLARS

Pessimism is out of place in the presence of the promises of God. As the saying goes, "We cannot talk about standing on the Rock of Ages and then act as if we are clinging to our last piece of driftwood." Could our anxiety about the future reflect fear—the fear that we shall have to confess our own weaknesses and trust God in ways that are unfamiliar? Five unshakable pillars will provide a firm footing as we stand against the forces of our crumbling culture.

God Still Reigns

Sometimes God gives a leader to a nation who is *better* than that nation deserves. Josiah was a righteous king who tried to turn Judah back to God at a time when the nation had slid into rebellion and idolatry. "Josiah was eight years old when he became king, and he reigned in Jerusalem for thirty-one years . . . He did what was right in the eyes of the Lord" (2 Kings 22:1–2). Under his leadership the Book of the Law was found and read. The Passover was reinstituted. He removed witchcraft and occultism from the land.

But the nation had fallen so far into rebellion that those reforms barely delayed the coming judgment: "Nevertheless, the Lord did not turn away from the heat of his fierce anger, which burned against Judah because of all that Manasseh had done to arouse his anger" (2 Kings 23:26). The cultural currents of Manasseh were so powerful that Josiah and his reforms could not turn the nation back to God. Josiah was a better king than the nation deserved.

Sometimes a leader is *far worse* than the nation deserves. We would all agree that the people of the former Soviet Union did not deserve Stalin; the people of Germany did not deserve Hitler. During such times, God reveals the evil of the human heart for all to see. And even through wicked leaders He purifies His church and accomplishes His purposes.

Sometimes God gives a leader to a nation that it *does* deserve. In the days of the Judges the people of Israel clamored for a king so they could be like all the other nations. God had other plans. But when the godly prophet Samuel prayed about the situation, the Lord replied, "Listen to all that the people are saying to you; it is not you they have rejected, but they have rejected me as their king" (1 Samuel 8:7). So God gave them exactly what they wanted, a king after their own liking. Saul was anointed as the first king of the nation, and, due to his disobedience, Israel suffered. Saul was a rather accurate reflection of the people themselves. He was exactly what the nation deserved.

Yet in each of these instances God was in control. He does not do what is evil, of course, nor are people programmed like a computer to do His will. People choose; they do what they like or what seems best at the moment. Yet, through secondary causes, they act under the providential hand of God. That is why Daniel could write that "the Most High is sovereign over all kingdoms on earth and gives them to anyone he wishes and sets over them the lowliest of people" (Daniel 4:17).

The actions of a king, court, or president will never thwart the plan of God. No matter what evil plans are hatched on earth, "The One enthroned in heaven laughs; the Lord scoffs at them" (Psalm 2:4). Whether the leader is Nero, George Washington, or President Morsi in Egypt, "there is no authority except that which God has established. The authorities that exist have been established by God" (Romans 13:1). Pilate, you will remember, had no power at all against Jesus, except "what was given to him from above."

Knowing this, we do not have to run and hide. We can embrace our present circumstances; we can pray for those who are in authority and we can depend on God for the wisdom we need to make a difference in the here and now. We were called for this moment, and therefore we must remember that *the task ahead of us is never as great as the Power behind us.*

Our God reigns!!!

The Church Is Still Precious

Hitler never discouraged anyone from attending church, just as long as the Christianity they accepted would not interfere with his agenda for Germany and the world. In other words, as long as the church was weak, freighted, and fragmented enough to be co-opted for his purposes, the dictator did not much mind the existence of the church. Thankfully, there were many believers who refused to be co-opted, and they paid a heavy price; for many, it meant death in a concentration camp.

God has given sufficient resources to His people that we do not have to be co-opted by politicians, by the world, or the pressures of our culture! Most of the letters of the New Testament were written to teach Christians how to be victorious even as they suffered. The church is to be a transformational community even when it has no political power, when it is falsely accused, and openly persecuted by pagans.

Put yourself in a time machine and go back

to the first century, when the common people had no part in selecting their leaders. As a Christian you are harassed for your faith in accordance with government policy. You are shunned in the marketplace. Your children are ridiculed as they play or work in the fields. You are constantly faced with questions: what is essential to my faith; what is not? Some of your friends who are outspoken about their faith are executed. Others remain silent, keeping their faith to themselves. How are you to survive in a pagan culture? Your loyalty to Christ and loyalty to the state are in constant conflict.

To those who actually lived under such oppression, Peter, who himself eventually died for his faith, wrote, "But you are a chosen people, a royal priesthood, a holy nation, God's special possession, that you may declare the praises of him who called you out of darkness into his wonderful light" (1 Peter 2:9).

What follows are detailed instructions on how God would have us live within a hostile culture. But before the church can *do*, it must *be*. If we are not holy, we cannot be salt and light to society. We dare not think that we can substitute politics for purity. Knowing who we are gives us the courage to live as we should. Our roots must be firmly planted in our unchangeable relationship with God before we are prepared to live in this changeable culture.

First, *we are a chosen race.* That is, we were chosen in Christ before the foundation of the world, and even then our names were written in heaven (Revelation 13:8). The knowledge that we are precious to God inspires us to live up to our calling. God is not about to abandon us because we feel weak politically or unpopular in our culture.

Second, *we are a royal priesthood.* In the Old Testament era the high priest could go into the Holy of Holies only one day a year. Today, we who are believers actually live in the Holy of Holies, for Christ has brought us into God's presence and left us there. For this reason we need never think that God has abandoned His people. When confronted with a hostile culture, we can daily come before God to receive grace to help in the time of need. *The greater the need, the greater the grace.*

Third, *we are a holy nation*—that is, we are set apart to God. We should be astonished if the world welcomed our moral and political agenda. Christ exposes the sins of the world, and darkness loves darkness.

The church is to be in the world as a ship is in the ocean—but when the ocean gets into the ship it begins to take on water. If it is true that (as polls suggest) the basic lifestyle of believers today is essentially no different from that of the world, why should we be surprised if our impact in this culture is so limited?

Finally, *we are, above all, a people for God's own possession.* No matter what personal battles we may face, we are still number one on God's list of priorities. We are the objects of His attention; He is preparing us to eternally display His grace and wisdom (Ephesians 2:7).

Such a calling should not fill us with pride but with humility. We should consider it an honor to be identified with Christ. Special blessings come with duly earned persecution.

Our calling is to live out the reality of who we are with dignity, kindness, and conviction. If we confront the world in anger or needlessly antagonize, we have abandoned our calling. We are to model the character of Christ in a world that is skeptical, a world that is convinced that God doesn't matter.

As believers we can be sure that *there is no such thing as meaningless suffering.* After all, we are God's special possession.

Our Mission Is Still Clear

What should we be doing? Peter says that we are to "declare the praises of him who called you out of darkness into his wonderful light" (1 Peter 2:9). Remember, this was written to those who were targeted by the pagans for special harassment. Just as flowers sometimes do not emit their fragrance unless they are crushed, so believers often do not exude the beauty of Christ unless they feel the pressure of the world. No matter the political regime or the hostility of the culture, believers are to make Christ attractive to the world.

Sadly, so often our churches are abandoning the very gospel message this nation needs to hear. Years ago I read a book on how England, which was at one time a Christian country, became the atheistic country it is today. The author explained that there was a time when "the cross was still preached but it was so bedecked with flowers that no one could see it." Today the message of the cross, which is "the Gospel unto salvation," is bedecked with the flowers of health and wealth and positive thinking. As the years progress, we can expect more pressure to dumb down, dilute, or otherwise minimize the message of the Gospel. Let us never be satisfied with a shallow Gospel that appeals to the lowest common denominator but does not transform the human heart.

First, *we represent Christ by our lifestyles.* "Live such good lives among the pagans that, though they accuse you of doing wrong, they may see your good deeds and glorify God on the day he visits us" (1 Peter 2:12).

We are to continue doing good deeds no matter how intense the pressure becomes. If we, like the Pharisees, stand in judgment on our culture without an honest sense of our own failures, if we see the world as our enemy and act as though we have not contributed to our cultural drift, we lose credibility.

Why is the world so smug in its unbelief? It has lost faith in the believability of God. Most people have not seen a credible Christian witness, a model of what a person in whom God is alive and working is like. They have seen angry, judgmental Christians; they have seen inconsistent Christians; and they have seen scandals that have revealed some ministers to be brazen hypocrites. Is it any wonder that they dismiss our faith? Humanly speaking, there may be powerful reasons why the world does not believe.

Bishop Samuel, who died in a hail of gunfire when Anwar Sadat was killed in the early '70s, told a friend of mine how Christianity swept across North Africa in the early centuries. The Christians were persecuted and had the most demeaning jobs, like garbage collection, for instance. When the plagues came the pagans burned the bodies, but the Christians would wash them and give them a decent burial, arguing that given the resurrection even pagans had a right to a decent burial. In fact, Cyprian (died AD 258) said that Christianity would never have spread but for the plagues because Christians died differently; they had the hope of being reunited. The pagans said of the Christians, "they carried their dead as if in triumph."

When abandoned babies were left out on the streets and back alleys, the Christians in North Africa organized baby runs and brought these babies to nursing mothers. The pagans were overwhelmed with the caring attitude of the Christians. Just as Peter predicted, unbelievers were led to faith in Christ and "glorified God" in the day of visitation.

The excellencies of Christ are best revealed through the lives of those who are compassionate because they themselves are profoundly aware of their own shortcomings. The world can out entertain us; outnumber us; out finance us, but let it never be said that they can out-love us, for "God has poured out his love into our hearts by the Holy Spirit, whom he has given us" (Romans 5:5).

On every level the church must show itself as a redeemed community, filled with imperfect people who themselves struggle with all the failings of the world. The difference is that we have a new sense of identity as those who belong to God. We know both the reality of sin and the joy of grace. Let us remember that what the world needs most is *to see Jesus.*

A mission agency that monitors the church in the People's Republic of China asked thousands of believers what drew them to faith in Christ. Many answers were given, but one was listed most often: the joy in the lives of believers with whom they came in contact made them envious.

Second, *we must win the intellectual and moral war through loving confrontation and persuasiveness.* Peter wrote, "But in your hearts revere Christ as Lord. Always be prepared to give an answer to everyone who asks you to give the reason for the hope that you have" (1 Peter 3:15).

Apologetics, the defense of the faith, must change its focus. At one time apologetics was a study that showed the superiority of Christianity over other religions. Today the Bible is vilified as being socially repressive, accused of teaching slavery and the subjugation of women. So today, apologetics must be taught as a coherent defense of the Christian worldview, along with answers to specific attacks against Christianity. We must be able to discuss all aspects of Christianity in a reasonable, believable way, trusting the Holy Spirit for wisdom and to empower us to defend the Gospel.

It would be a tragedy indeed if, as a result of the irreversible trends that I highlight in this booklet, we were to withdraw from the cultural debates and retreat behind the walls of our churches under the guise of being "faithful." Of course God wants us to be "faithful," but that faithfulness includes involvement in all levels of culture, including politics, the media, education, and the like.

All of the evidence is on our side in the war of ideas that rages in America today. We have excellent reasons to believe that Christ is superior to all of the other religious leaders of the world. Whether it is opposition to abortion or same-sex marriage, or to argue for the positive role of religion in public life—all of these convictions can be well defended. In fact, we can show that without a belief in God there can be no morality whatsoever. At a most basic level, every believer should be trained to share the Gospel, the very heart of Christianity.

Third, *we must do all we can to strengthen our families.* The future stability of America is dependent on a commitment to marriage and the teaching of children. Many parents are removing their children from the public school system, disappointed at what is being taught and the behavior tolerated. Thus the homeschool movement is growing. Other parents are working actively on school boards and in their PTAs, trying to make their schools what they should be. I'm convinced that those parents who truly seek God regarding these kinds of decisions will receive guidance from the Lord. Remember, God takes special interest in His people.

Author and social critic Os Guinness has warned that when we begin to feel sorry for ourselves we must remember "that the effect of playing the victim is to reject the ethic of Christ and resort to a politics of resentment. The politics of resentment is the politics of revenge." We are not a majority, but God keep us from becoming an angry, vindictive minority! Self-pity loses sight of the promises of God and leads to a mindset of withdrawal, an attitude that says, "Since they hate us, let them rot." How unlike our Master!

As the late Charles Colson put it, "Our place is on our knees, in the streets helping people in need, winning our neighbors and colleagues to a Christian worldview by speaking the truth in love. We will win the cultural war one house, one block at a time, as God's people are trained and equipped by the church and then go out and live their faith in the world."

Never before in American history has it been so important to become an active part of a network of other believers for worship, encouragement, instruction, and prayer. Bible studies, prayer groups, and discipleship training of believers to be change-agents in their world.

The day of the casual Christian is over. No longer is it possible to drift along, hoping that no tough choices will have to be made. At this point in American history, any moral and spiritual progress will have to be won at great cost. The darker the night, the more important every candle becomes.

Our Focus Is Still Heaven

Years ago we heard the cliché, "Some people are so heavenly minded that they are no earthly good." My observation is that this no longer applies today. Most of us are so earthly minded that we are no heavenly good! The pressures of life have led us to borrow the values of the world.

Peter writes, "Dear friends, I urge you, as foreigners and exiles, to abstain from sinful desires, which wage war against your soul" (1 Peter 2:11). Strangers and aliens understand their present surroundings and know where they are headed.

First, *we must see this world as temporary.* Many of us are not meaningfully involved in our political and moral battles until we ourselves are affected. As Francis Schaeffer told us decades ago, the primary desire of most American Christians is "to live in personal peace and affluence." If we are not on the front lines, we may become indifferent to others who are engulfed in the cultural battles that erupt around us.

The apostle Paul taught that the real world was not the cosmos, but that there is an eternal, unchanging, and unseen world to which we are headed. Pilgrims who pass through a territory en route to their permanent home do not drive in their stakes too deeply. They know they are leaving in the morning.

Second, *we need to reaffirm our faith in the fact of the return of Christ and His triumph in the world.* Yes, it is true that the church has been awaiting the return of Christ for 2,000 years and He has as yet not come. However, even if He does not return in our lifetime, when He does return we will be raised to be with Him forever.

On July 4, 1952, thirty-four-year-old Florence Chadwick waded into the water at Catalina Island, hoping to be the first woman to swim the twenty-one-mile strait to California. The water was numbingly cold and the fog so thick that she could not even see the boats in her own party. As the hours ticked by she swam on, but fifteen hours later, numbed by the cold, she asked to be taken out of the water. Within a few moments she realized that she was within a half mile from the shore. She regretted giving up, saying, "if only I would have been able to see the shore, I could have made it."

However, two years later, though the weather was the same, she did succeed in swimming the strait; the reason, she said, was "I always kept the image of the shoreline in my mind."

When we are discouraged, let's resolve to keep the eternal shoreline in mind! Our eventual triumph is assured. We have read the last chapter of the book; we know how it all will end.

Meanwhile, en route to heaven, we should not think it strange when we hear that the secular press is biased against the Christian faith. We should not think it strange when the police arrest

Christians who are using a public park for prayer.

We think these things are strange because we have forgotten that such treatment should be expected as part of our calling. To quote Peter once more:

> Dear friends, do not be surprised at the fiery ordeal that has come on you to test you, as though something strange were happening to you. But rejoice inasmuch as you participate in the sufferings of Christ, so that you may be overjoyed when his glory is revealed. If you are insulted because of the name of Christ, you are blessed, for the Spirit of glory and of God rests on you. If you suffer, it should not be as a murderer or thief or any other kind of criminal, or even as a meddler. However, if you suffer as a Christian, do not be ashamed, but praise God that you bear that name. (1 Peter 4:12–16)

Finally—and most important—Peter tells us exactly what we should do when we are being persecuted for our faith. When we are a minority, when all hope for changes seems to be gone and we are faced with no political, judicial, or financial power, "So, then, those who suffer according to God's will should commit themselves to their faithful Creator and continue to do good" (4:19).

The best example of how to handle persecution comes from the first-century Christians who had their property confiscated and then were thrown into jail for their faith. How did they react? "You . . . joyfully accepted the confiscation of your property, because you knew that you yourselves had better and lasting possessions" (Hebrews 10:34). They accepted the seizure of their property and even imprisonment with joy because they knew where their real home and future lay.

Time is short, eternity is long. Heaven is just around the next corner.

God Still Answers Prayer

Satan is not more powerful today than he was in the past. He is, however, more visible, especially when the church retreats from meaningful engagement with the world. Satan is especially visible when the church acts on its own initiative without active faith in God.

On several occasions I've been in the so-called Luther Room in the Wartburg Castle in Germany. There, living the life of a hermit, Luther translated the entire New Testament into German in just six weeks! But it is also there, tradition says, he threw an inkwell at the devil. Indeed, tour guides used to rub a bit of soot on the wall, because tourists wanted to see where the inkwell landed!

If Luther did indeed throw his inkwell at the devil I'm sure that the devil was not perturbed. No evil spirit would fear an inkwell coming in his direction, even if it were thrown with accuracy and speed. No demon would duck, hoping it would miss its target. In fact, I'm not convinced that Luther threw an inkwell at the devil at all. In his Table Talks he says he "fought the devil with ink," meaning his work translating the New Testament into German. That's the way to fight the devil: *put the Bible into the hands of the populace*!

We must not spend our time "throwing inkwells at the devil," so to speak. You can't fight a spiritual being with physical weapons! Physical battles are fought with physical weapons, spiritual battles with spiritual weapons.

At root we must remember that our battle in America at the most basic level is spiritual, not political or even moral. Thus, although we use all the opportunities at our disposal to stand against the trends of our culture, we might still just be throwing inkwells at the devil. Politics, cultural involvement, and witnessing to our faith are incredibly important, certainly more effective than throwing an inkwell at the devil. But they in themselves will not stand against our irreversible cultural currents.

In short, we must pray, but not just any kind of prayer will do. We must be prepared to deal radically with sin and meet the requirements of heartfelt repentance. We usually think that God is obligated to come to our deliverance; we think that God is obligated to reverse our cultural trends so that we can return to better days. However, in the Old Testament, God said these startling words to His chosen people: "Yet they rebelled and grieved his Holy Spirit. So he turned and became their enemy and he himself fought against them" (Isaiah 63:10). In other words, there are times when God no longer takes up the cause of His people. When we refuse to repent of our own sins, God might refuse to come to our aid and let us be defeated. This is why we must turn to Him as families, as churches, and as individuals. Without repentance for our own sins, we cannot expect to win our cultural wars.

Never have we needed God's intervention so desperately; never before have we felt so helpless in the face of a massive national movements that we cannot stop. Ours is a battle that cannot be won by reason, scientific data, or dialogue, though, as I argued above, they have value in their own spheres. We must in desperation call on God for deliverance and the strength to weather the storms that have already begun to come our way.

One day the king Jehoshaphat woke up and was told that a vast army was coming against him. The king consulted God about what to do and proclaimed a fast throughout the land of Judah. The people then gathered from every town in the land to seek help from the Lord. Jehoshaphat then stood in the temple of the Lord, and prayed.

> Lord, the God of our ancestors, are you not the God who is in heaven? You rule over all the kingdoms of the nations. Power and might are in your hand, and no one can withstand you. Our God, did you not drive out the inhabitants of this land before your people Israel and give it forever to the descendants of Abraham your friend? . . . If calamity comes upon us, whether the sword of judgment, or plague or famine, we will stand in your presence before this temple that bears your Name and will cry out to you in our distress, and you will hear and save us . . . Our God, will you not judge them [the adversaries]? *For we have no power to face this vast army that is attacking us. We do not know what to do, but our eyes are*

upon you. (2 Chronicles 20:6-7; 9; 12, emphasis added)

We do not know what to do, but our eyes are upon You!

I wonder what would happen if millions of believers set aside their schedules to seek God on behalf of this nation . . .

I wonder what would happen if privately and corporately we confessed our sins and turned away from our own idols . . .

I wonder if perhaps God would intervene so the destruction of marriages and the forces that seek to tear our families apart would be stayed.

Back to Jehoshaphat: Through a man anointed with the Spirit, the word of the Lord came, "Do not be afraid or discouraged because of this vast army. For the battle is not yours, but God's" (v.15). Then the king commanded that a select group of men walk ahead of the army singing and praising God for the splendor of His holiness. And God gave the victory!

Please understand that God does not owe us such a deliverance. No nation has turned away from so much light in order to choose darkness. No nation has squandered as many opportunities as we have. We can only call on God for mercy, and if it pleases Him He will come to our aid. We certainly cannot expect a revival simply because we do not want to face the harassment that well might come to us all. But if we humble ourselves, weeping for this nation, God may yet intervene and restore decency to this crazed world. Most of all, we should pray that millions would be converted and belong to God forever. People change their minds only when God changes their hearts.

Will America turn back to a belief in biblical absolutes? Will the freedom of speech return to our classrooms? Will traditional marriage be upheld in our society? We simply do not know the answers. God may graciously intervene and send this nation to its knees. G. K. Chesterton said, "At least five times the Faith has to all appearance gone to the dogs. In each of these five cases, it was the dog that died."

On the other hand, America may continue to self-destruct, headed for moral oblivion. Whether or not we win this cultural war is really up to God; whether we are faithful is, to a large extent, up to us. The essential truth is that *God has given us all the resources we need to be all that we should be for us glory at this moment in history*.

But if we cannot weep before God, we are probably not fit to fight before men. Let me encourage you to become a part of OneCry, a growing prayer movement that will not only connect you with other believers, but will give you encouragement and resources to call on God with others during this critical hour of history. Sign on to their Declaration of Spiritual Emergency and join all those of us who believe that prayer—desperate prayer—is our only real hope. Simply go to www.onecry.com.

Only God can save us now.

MOTIVATED BY ANOTHER WORLD

We've already emphasized that we do not need freedom of religion in order to be faithful to our calling. Just read *The Voice of the Martyrs* magazine and think of the number of Christians being martyred, especially throughout the Middle East, for the cause of the Gospel. They are led away as "sheep to be slaughtered," as the apostle Paul put it, and God has not given them deliverance. Their faith is most honoring to God, and they are an example to us.

We do not have to be victorious in this world to triumph in the next. We do not accept the world's philosophy that we have to have it all now or we will never have another chance. We do not have to seek retaliation for all the personal injustices we might experience in this life. *We believe in another world.*

During the terrible Boxer Rebellion in China at the turn of the previous century (the leaders were so nicknamed because they practiced gymnastics and calisthenics), the "boxers" captured a mission station, then placed a flat cross on the ground. They gave instruction that those who trampled the cross as they came out of the building would be set free; those who walked around the cross, honoring it, would be executed. The first seven students trampled the cross under their feet and were released. But the eighth student, a young girl, knelt beside the cross and prayed for strength. Then she slowly walked around the cross to face the firing squad. Strengthened by her example, every one of the more than ninety other students followed her to death. Did they win?

Throughout history during times of oppression the sole cry of believers has almost always been to God. Without spite, revenge, and hostility, they, like their Master, believed that they were called to pay the ultimate price. Often they remained calm and forgiving.

Losers? Yes, from the standpoint of this world. But they belonged to another world where they were winners indeed. Christ himself appeared to be a loser if we look only at the cross and fail to see the resurrection and ascension. We dare not judge success by months, days, or years, but by eternity. In the end every tongue will give God glory, "that at the name of Jesus every knee should bow, in heaven and on earth and under the earth, and every tongue acknowledge that Jesus Christ is Lord, to the glory of God the Father" (Philippians 2:10–11).

"It is better to fail at a cause that will ultimately succeed than to succeed in a cause that will ultimately fail," wrote the late Peter Marshall, minister and US Senate chaplain. Better to be faithful in building the church than to succeed at something that doesn't really matter.

COMMITMENT UNTO DEATH

I've been told that after a young African was martyred for his faith, this writing was found in his room; here is an excerpt:

> I'm part of the fellowship of the unashamed, the die has been cast, I have stepped over the line, the decision has been made—I'm a disciple of Jesus Christ—I won't look back, let us, slow down, back away or be still.
>
> My past is redeemed, my present makes

sense, my future is secure—I'm finished and done with low living, sight walking, smooth knees, colorless dreams, tamed visions, worldly talking, cheap giving and dwarfed goals.

My pace is set, my gait is fast, my goal is heaven, my road is narrow, my way is rough, my companions are few, my guide is reliable, my mission is clear. I won't give up, shut up, let up until I have stayed up, stored up, prayed up for the cause of Jesus Christ.

I must go till He comes, give till I drop, preach till everyone knows, work till He stops me and when He comes for His own, He will have no trouble recognizing me because my banner will have been clear.

With this kind of resolve we will, with God's help, have the strength to withstand our crumbling culture, and perhaps even reverse what seems to be "irreversible." Of course, we are a minority, but armed with the promises of God we can have a spiritual impact that is greater than our numbers might suggest.

It may come down to a simple question: *Are we willing to pay the price?*

NOTES

1. *Chicago Tribune*, "Illinois' state debt climbs to $21,607 per person," October 2, 2012. http://articles. chicagotribune.com/2012-10-02/business/chi-state-debt-per-capita-falls-to-13425-20121002_1_ state-debt-state-budget-solutions-pension-liability.

2. See the documentary film *IndoctriNation: Public Schools and the Decline of Christianity in America.*

3. Todd Starnes, "Court Says Gay Rights Trump Religious Rights," *FOX News & Commentary*, June 5, 2012. http://radio.foxnews.com/toddstarnes/top-stories/court-says-gay-rights-trump-religious-rights.html.

4. Fran Spielman, "Emanuel goes after Chick-fil-A for boss' anti-gay views," *Chicago Sun-Times*, July 25, 2012. http://www.suntimes.com/news/cityhall/13988905-418/ald-moreno-trying-to-block-new-chick-fil-a-over-boss-stance-on-gay-marriage.html.

5. Annie Linskey, "Gallaudet official suspended for signing anti-same-sex marriage petition," *The Baltimore Sun*, October 10, 2012. http://articles.baltimoresun.com/2012-10-10/news/bal-gallaudet-official-suspended-for-signing-anti-samesex-marriage-petition-20121010_1_marriage-law-maryland-marriage-alliance-marriage-petition.

6. See Erwin W. Lutzer, *The Cross in the Shadow of the Crescent: An Informed Response to Islam's War with Christianity* (Eugene, OR: Harvest House, 2012).

MORE TITLES
BY ERWIN LUTZER

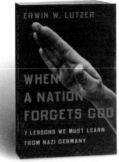

978-0-8024-4656-5

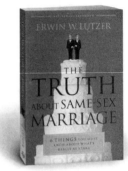

978-0-8024-9177-0

WHEN A NATION FORGETS GOD

Erwin Lutzer tells us we must take note of lessons from the Nazi regime in history and be vigilant in our stand for truth, justice, and righteousness.

THE TRUTH ABOUT SAME-SEX MARRIAGE

Is marriage still the sacred bond between a man and a woman? Understand what the Bible really has to say about the topic of homosexuality, and learn how to approach this difficult issue with dignity and sensitivity.

Also available as an ebook

MOODY
PUBLISHERS

www.MoodyPublishers.com

MORE TITLES
BY ERWIN LUTZER

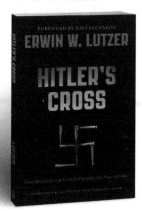

978-0-8024-0850-1   978-0-8024-6308-1

ONE MINUTE AFTER YOU DIE

Many people spend more time planning for a vacation than preparing for eternity. This classic makes an encouraging gift for believers and a tasteful word of caution for the undecided.

HITLER'S CROSS

Erwin Lutzer traces Hitler's rise to power, reveals the role of the church in Germany's tragedy, and issues a warning about what could happen to America.

Also available as an ebook

www.MoodyPublishers.com

On November 25th, 2012,
Erwin Lutzer preached,
"Where Do We Go
from Here?"
to his congregation at Moody Church in Chicago, IL.
This book is based on this sermon. Scan the QR code
or visit the link below to watch the video.

www.moodychurch.org/watch-online/where-do-we-go-here/

MOODY
PUBLISHERS
www.MoodyPublishers.com

A Nationwide Call for Spiritual Awakening

TAKE THE NEXT STEP
IN BRINGING RENEWAL TO AMERICA

Sign the OneCry Declaration of Spiritual
Emergency at **onecry.com**.

www.onecry.com

www.MoodyPublishers.com